Little People, BIG DREAMS™
SIMONE BILES

Written by
Maria Isabel Sánchez Vegara

Illustrated by
Nadia Fisher

Frances Lincoln
Children's Books

Once in Ohio lived a tiny girl who couldn't keep still.
Her name was Simone. When she was three, Simone and
her sister went to Texas to live with their grandparents.

Jumping on the trampoline and doing flips off furniture was her favorite game. Simone grew so close to her grandparents that she decided to call them Mom and Dad. They taught her to never take things for granted and always try her best.

One day, Simone went on a field trip to a gym. When she saw the gymnasts exercising, Simone copied them. The coaches were so amazed by her talent that they wrote a note to her family asking them to sign her up.

Her grandparents knew it was a chance for little Simone to fly—and it would give their sofa a break! As soon as she started training, she proved she had the qualities of a great gymnast: strength, flexibility, balance, and grace.

For years, Simone did her best at the gym. She mastered all four gymnastic events: vault, uneven bars, balance beam, and her favorite, floor exercise. She was fourteen when she earned her spot on the senior U.S. team.

Simone became the first African American gymnast to win an all-around title at the World Championships. She was also the first female U.S. gymnast to win four gold medals and a bronze at a single Olympic Games, including one with her team!

However, Simone and her teammates achieved one of their greatest victories away from the sport.

When they bravely spoke up about the things adults in charge of the team were doing wrong, they realized that together they were strong!

Simone continued piling up medals and setting new goals in her journal. She became the first woman to successfully land a "Yurchenko Double Pike" in a U.S. competition, the most challenging women's vault with the highest difficulty score.

2x

That year, at the Tokyo Olympics, the eyes of the world and the hopes of a nation were on her. The pressure to go out there and do what people expected of her was huge, and Simone didn't want to disappoint anyone.

Simone was performing a vault when she noticed that her mind and body were struggling to work as one. No one loved gymnastics as much as her, but she knew it was time to step back and put her health ahead of the sport.

Back home, Simone found time to enjoy all the other good things she loved in life, like being a daughter, wife, and friend. She was also a role model for young athletes who felt overwhelmed by the stress of reaching the top.

THE GREATEST OF ALL TIME

When she felt ready to return, she did it wrapped in glitter, sequins, and self-belief. At age twenty-six, she became the oldest woman to win a national all-around title and the only woman to do so eight times.

And crowds will keep cheering for Simone. Not only because she is the greatest gymnast ever, but because she is the girl she has always been: a little storm with the belief that there is gold in all of us.

SIMONE BILES

(Born 1997)

2012

2016

Simone Arianne Biles was born in Ohio. When her mother became unable to look after Simone and her siblings, the children moved into foster care. A few years later, Simone's older siblings went to live with their great aunt and she and her younger sister were adopted by their grandparents. In her new home in Texas, she felt safe and loved. Simone's gymnastics journey began with a trip to a local gym, where she started copying older children practicing their moves. Coaches spotted her natural talent, and she spent the next eleven years training at Bannon's Gymnastix, a gymnastics academy. During this time, doctors discovered she had a medical condition called attention deficit hyperactivity disorder (ADHD). Simone had been finding school difficult and this diagnosis helped

2019

2022

her understand why. With support from her family and professionals, she kept following her dreams. As a teenager, she competed at an elite level with great success and won four gold medals at the Olympic Games in Rio. Over the next few years, a flurry of medals and records secured Simone's status as "The Greatest of All Time." In gymnastics, a move is named after the person who is the first to perform it at a big, international competition, and Simone has five named after her! As well as being the first American woman to win eight national all-around titles, she has received the Presidential Medal of Freedom and is a passionate mental-health advocate. Simone believes that "before you can achieve, you must believe in yourself," a message that her story shows is true.

Want to find out more?

Have a read of this great book:

40 Inspiring Icons: Amazing Athletes by Jean-Michel Billioud and Gonoh

With help from an adult, you can watch Simone's amazing routines online.

Published by Peter Marley · Designed by Lyli Feng
Commissioned by Lucy Menzies · Edited by Molly Mead and Rachel Robinson
Production by Nikki Ingram

Manufactured by Corporate Graphics USA, 092024
3 5 7 9 8 6 4 2

Photographic acknowledgments (pages 28-29, from left to right): 1. All-around winner Simone Biles waves to crowd with 2nd place Madison Desch and 3rd place Amelia Hundley © ZUMA Press, Inc. via Alamy Stock Photo. 2. American gymnast Simone Biles competes in the floor routine qualifications at the 2016 Rio Summer Olympics in Rio de Janeiro, Brazil, August 6, 2016 © Kevin Dietsch/UPI via Alamy Stock Photo. 3. Photo taken Oct. 13, 2019, shows Simone Biles of the United States after winning five gold medals at the world gymnastics championships in Stuttgart, Germany © Kyodo News via Getty Images. 4. WASHINGTON, DC – JULY 7: U.S. President Joe Biden presents the Presidential Medal of Freedom to Simone Biles © Alex Wong via Getty Images.

FSC MIX
Supporting responsible forestry
FSC® C008080

Collect the *Little People,* **BIG DREAMS**™ series:

FRIDA KAHLO	COCO CHANEL	MAYA ANGELOU	AMELIA EARHART	AGATHA CHRISTIE	MARIE CURIE	ROSA PARKS	AUDREY HEPBURN	EMMELINE PANKHURST
ELLA FITZGERALD	ADA LOVELACE	JANE AUSTEN	GEORGIA O'KEEFFE	HARRIET TUBMAN	ANNE FRANK	MOTHER TERESA	JOSEPHINE BAKER	L. M. MONTGOMERY
JANE GOODALL	SIMONE DE BEAUVOIR	MUHAMMAD ALI	STEPHEN HAWKING	MARIA MONTESSORI	VIVIENNE WESTWOOD	MAHATMA GANDHI	DAVID BOWIE	WILMA RUDOLPH
DOLLY PARTON	BRUCE LEE	RUDOLF NUREYEV	ZAHA HADID	MARY SHELLEY	MARTIN LUTHER KING JR.	DAVID ATTENBOROUGH	ASTRID LINDGREN	EVONNE GOOLAGONG
BOB DYLAN	ALAN TURING	BILLIE JEAN KING	GRETA THUNBERG	JESSE OWENS	JEAN-MICHEL BASQUIAT	ARETHA FRANKLIN	CORAZON AQUINO	PELÉ
ERNEST SHACKLETON	STEVE JOBS	AYRTON SENNA	LOUISE BOURGEOIS	ELTON JOHN	JOHN LENNON	PRINCE	CHARLES DARWIN	CAPTAIN TOM MOORE
HANS CHRISTIAN ANDERSEN	STEVIE WONDER	MEGAN RAPINOE	MARY ANNING	MALALA YOUSAFZAI	ANDY WARHOL	RUPAUL	MICHELLE OBAMA	MINDY KALING

IRIS APFEL	ROSALIND FRANKLIN	RUTH BADER GINSBURG	MARILYN MONROE	KAMALA HARRIS	ALBERT EINSTEIN	CHARLES DICKENS	YOKO ONO	MICHAEL JORDAN

NELSON MANDELA	PABLO PICASSO	AMANDA GORMAN	GLORIA STEINEM	FLORENCE NIGHTINGALE	HARRY HOUDINI	J.R.R. TOLKIEN	ELVIS PRESLEY	NEIL ARMSTRONG

ALEXANDER VON HUMBOLDT	NIKOLA TESLA	WILMA MANKILLER	MARCUS RASHFORD	LAVERNE COX	MAE JEMISON	DWAYNE JOHNSON	HELEN KELLER	ANNA PAVLOVA

QUEEN ELIZABETH	TERRY FOX	HEDY LAMARR	SHAKIRA	FREDDIE MERCURY	LEWIS HAMILTON	LOUIS PASTEUR	PRINCESS DIANA	DAVID HOCKNEY

VANESSA NAKATE	OLIVE MORRIS	KING CHARLES	MOZART	STEVE IRWIN	JÜRGEN KLOPP	LEO MESSI	SALLY RIDE	TENZING NORGAY

KYLIE MINOGUE	BEYONCÉ	TAYLOR SWIFT	RAFA NADAL	USAIN BOLT	SIMONE BILES	STAN LEE	LEONARD COHEN	VINCENT VAN GOGH

MARY KOM	SALVADOR DALÍ	ANTOINE DE SAINT-EXUPÉRY	DAVID BECKHAM	KATHERINE JOHNSON	YAYOI KUSAMA

Scan the QR code for free activity sheets, teachers' notes and more information about the series at www.littlepeoplebigdreams.com